# The Adventures of Frenchy the Little Red Fox and his Friends

## Volume 2

# Puppies and Piggies Around the Farm

**Frenchy the Fox - Books for Kids Series**

By Monica Wagner and Christian Stahl

First published in Great Britain in 2022 by Midealuck Publishing Ltd.

The right of Christian J. Stahl to be identified as the Author of the work has been asserted by him in accordance with the Copyright.

**All rights reserved.**

No part of this publication may be reproduced, stored in a retrieval system, or transmitted, in any form or by any means without prior written permission of the publisher, nor be otherwise circulated in any form of binding or cover than that in which it is published and without similar condition being imposed on the subsequent purchaser. Midealuck Publishing Ltd. is responsible for the content and operation of this publication.

Any name and content in this book is fiction and not related to any real person or event.

**Table of Contents**

New Piggies on the Farm

Puppies and Piggies and the Disappeared Friends

The Snooping Contest

Frenchy and the Beaver

The Burrow

The Mink Farm

Walking on Thin Ice

Frenchy and the Squirrel

Barking Dogs

**New Piggies on the Farm**

Today, Frenchy the Fox wanted to get to the bottom of an old secret, and it all started on this mysterious farm on the forest's edge. On this farm, from time to time, but especially in the spring, many small young animals were born, and most of them were pigs. What Frenchy always noticed was that the young animals stayed with their mothers only for a few months, sometimes longer, but then, like a strange mystery, many of the little piggies disappeared overnight.

Today was the perfect day to investigate this matter; it was a cool sunny morning when Frenchy climbed on a high fence from where he had a clear view of what was happening on the farm.

Frenchy had gotten a hint from his friend Emma the goose, that strange things were happening on this farm and she had just spread the news that the big mother pig had new piggies in the sty. And all the other pigs were nervous; they told all the animals that they were very afraid, that soon some piggies would disappear again. The older pigs had already noticed that sometimes the farmer came into the sty and marked the little piggies with color.

And so it happened that just recently, four little piggies were born, they lay in the tiled pigsty and were suckled from dawn to dusk by the big mother pig.

This morning, Frenchy was sitting on the fence when suddenly a little pig came running from the pigsty right to the fence where Frenchy was on the lookout.

"Frenchy," cried the little pig, "tonight the farmer has taken another very young pig away!"

"Do you know which way the farmer went?"

"I think he carried the piggy into the hall there at the end of the farm."

Frenchy jumped off the fence and ran as fast as he could to the big hall. He stopped in front of the locked entrance, from the inside he heard a loud squeal. *What was going on*? Suddenly a dog barked, and through the crack in the gate Frenchy recognized an old shepherd dog, actually they had known each other for many years; the dog also recognized Frenchy and both sat down close to the gate and greeted each other. "Hey Frenchy, what are you doing here, the farmer is in here."

"I know," Frenchy replies. "That's why I'm here, I need to find something out."

"Well, I'm supposed to be watching the gate here," says the dog.

"Tell me my friend, is there a secret going on in there?"

"What kind of secret are you looking for?"

"Is there something going on with the young piggies?"

The dog nods sadly. "Yes, but I really don't want to tell you, because you are friends with the piggies."

Frenchy can sense his friend's sadness. "Is it really that bad?"

The dog nods and starts to cry.

Frenchy fears the worst. "Then I don't even want to know," he says, putting his paws over his eyes.

"Sometimes is better not to know everything." says the dog.

"That's right, we animals in the forest always say, we can eat everything, but we cannot know everything."

Sad and a little unsure, Frenchy sneaks out of the hall. The strange squealing from the inside makes him shiver.

When he finally returned to the pigsty the mother pig asks him if he has found out what happened to her little piggie.

Frenchy approaches the mother pig. "What do you think big Mother, what do you think do people to pigs?"

The mother just stared at him for a moment and then turned around and pushed the other piggies into a corner of the pigsty, she knew and kept her mouth shut, and since she accepted the things she couldn't change, she resigned herself to fate.

Frenchy did not want to continue the investigation, and in the end he wasn't quite sure what really happens to the pigs in the big hall, but maybe you know the answer.

.

**Puppies and Piggies and the Disappeared Friends**

Frenchy once knew a proud mother dog that was living in a barn on a farm, and had already a young family of puppies, but then she was pregnant again, and on a rainy morning in autumn, she gave birth to three little puppies, which looked like they were cut out of their mother's face. However, she gave birth to the little ones in a remote corner of the big pigsty, where there was a bit more quietness, instead of all the usual squealing of pigs, and yet the dogs were watched by the attentive big mother pig. However, the little puppies did not even pay any attention to the pigs; they loved to cuddle around and play with their siblings; they even occasionally wandered off and sniffed around the farm only to return quickly to the safe pigsty for food and comfort.

The next year, one day when the puppies had already reached half size, the mother dog gently pushed them out of the sty, every day a little more, because the puppies had to gradually learn to live outside on the farm and alone. Because, strictly speaking, they didn't like the pigs' food too much either, and the farmer fed all the animals on the farm pretty much the same food. But then again, the pigs seemed to be the most important animals on the farm. When some pigs were big and strong, the farmer led them to another barn, and what was going on there, we all did not know.

Actually, this was a very big farm where you could see all kinds of animals, including horses, sheep, cows, and many pigs, and in and around the farm there were dogs, mostly shepherd dogs, and the dogs were supposed to be watching the animals. However, the dogs were not always happy because the pigs were always the first to eat and the dogs were given the leftovers. With envy the dogs watched the other animals when they got fed first.

Eventually, the dogs got fed up and asked their friend Frenchy the fox if he could bring them a piece of meat once in a while. Frenchy was happy to help, but then again, it was never enough. Frenchy wasn't happy with the situation either, so he persuaded the dogs to gather every morning on the edge of the forest, there was actually always enough food, not necessarily meat but still better than what they could gather on the farm. But for the dogs, most of the time it was good enough because, after all, they were dogs and dogs eat just almost everything. But the truth was, the dogs were still a bit jealous of the other animals, especially the piggies.

One day the news went around that a big pig mother had given birth to several little piggies. Everyone on the farm liked the little piggies, and they were very attached to the mother. And after a few months, the little piggies had already grown considerably. The farmer brought the little piggies special food, actually he brought them little bags with special tasty treats in there, lumps that only animals like of course, and as a result of that the piggies seemed to grow even faster that way!

Of course, word spread quickly all over the farm that the little piggies were now getting a special treatment with special food only for them.

Even Frenchy got wind of it, and he as a sly and well-informed fox, sneaked one night into the pigsty just to have a little taste of the lumps.

He had just eaten the first piece when suddenly the big mother pig came squeaking running into the sty.

"Frenchy, what are you doing? That's our food!"

"I just wanted a taste!"

"The food is meant for the piggies!"

Frenchy looked curiously at the little piggies that were squatting timidly in the corner. "Hmm, your little piggies have grown very fast!"

"Yes, you're right about that, Frenchy."

"That's dangerous," Frenchy said.

"Dangerous? Why?"

Frenchy whispered in the mother pig's ear:

"When the piggies are big enough but still young, they'll be herded into another sty."

The mother pig recoiled a step, startled. "Oh, yes that's right. And what happens to the pigs there?"

Frenchy shrugged, "Nobody knows. But no pig has ever returned from there."

"Oh, my goodness. What can I do?"

Frenchy looked at the piggies, and then at the food, "I have an idea. I can take your piggies into the woods, they'll be safe there."

"Really? And who will watch them?"

"Can you still remember the puppies?"

"Oh yes, we love them all."

"See," Frenchy says a little proudly, "they have become big and strong, they'll take care of your babies."

The mother pig thought for a moment. "All right, I trust you, Frenchy. But will my little piggies have enough to eat there?"

Frenchy nodded his snout to the bags of treats.

"Come with me, you will see. Let's take all those bags, we'll drag them into the woods."

The mother pig whistled, and moments later, all the piggies and some other pigs started to carry the food bags to the edge of the forest. And they couldn't believe how happy the dogs were when the food bags finally arrived, which from that day on the piggies and puppies shared…more or less at least.

**The Snooping Contest**

Once on a big and beautiful farm on the edge of the forest lived a fast number of sheep, over a dozen cows, quite a lot of pigs, and even some dogs roamed happily around the farm.

The big black dogs belonged to the farm owner, an old man who actually owned the pig farm. The pigs mostly lived outside in an enclosure, but in winter, when it was very cold and especially when there was snow, they lived in a sty. This was also the place they were fed and where most of the pig babies were born.

Usually all the animals lived happily together, because each group of animals had its own area on the farm and its corner in the sty.

However, in that particular spring it was quite a busy time, because many new animal babies were born, including many puppies and piggies.

Since it was quite cold this spring morning, most of the animals stayed in the pigsties and pens, and the young piggies and puppies wanted to stay close to their mother who protected them from the elements and other animals.

Every morning, the farmer filled the feed troughs with fresh and tasty feed pellets. As soon as the containers were full, all the piggies ran as fast as they could to the troughs, and the mother pigs made sure that their piggies always came first. Actually, there was a whole row of feed cans, but then again, there were just as many pigs on the farm and the troughs had to be filled at least halfway to feed all the piggies. But on this spring morning, the young puppies were very hungry, but so were the piggies, and unfortunately for the dogs, the piggies were faster and stronger, they actually managed to push ahead of the puppies and ate from the troughs first. When they were finished eating, there was little food left in the troughs.

    Very sad and a bit angry, the three puppies trotted back to the corner of the sty, and the mother dog already suspected what had happened.

"Don't be sad, dear ones," said the mother dog. "When you're big, you'll definitely be faster to the troughs than the pigs."

"It can take a long time," said the youngest puppy.

"We need help, please help us," the sibling added.

"I can't do anything about it," said the dog mother, "The pigs are a bit bigger and I'm not allowed to interfere."

"Can't you find someone to help us?" asked the little one.

The dog mother lifted her head: "Wait a minute, maybe there is someone, I know a friend who is very smart."

All the puppies barked with excitement.

"Come on, little ones, I'll introduce you to someone."

A short time later, the mother dog and the puppies had gathered at the fence, and after a short bark, a small red fox actually appeared at the edge of the fence.

"This is my old friend, Frenchy the fox," said the dog mom.

She quickly explained her worries to Frenchy. French folded his arms, then stood on his hind legs.

"Maybe I can mediate," Frenchy suggested. "But I have to ask my friend about that, he's related to pigs."

"You also have a pig as a friend," the dog mother wanted to know.

"Well, actually, my friend is a wild boar, his name is Hugo, and he's as smart as he is good-natured."

"Dogs and foxes have to help each other," demanded the dog mother.

"That's what the mother pig could say about the foxes," Frenchy replied.

In order not to arouse suspicion, Frenchy the fox and Hugo the wild boar met at night near the end of the farm, on the edge of the forest.

Frenchy asked Hugo for advice, he also suggested his idea. His basic idea was that the pigs and the puppies should have a competition, maybe a race or something like that. The aim was that the puppies were also allowed to eat from the trough.

"So the puppies have to win," Hugo asked.

"Yes, they have to allow the puppies to eat from the same trough," Frenchy said.

"Well, I can imagine that."

"It is also important that the pigs participate."

Hugo: "I have an idea. We're doing a snooping competition. We hide truffles on the farm and whoever finds the truffles first gets to eat from the trough."

"Hopefully the puppies win then."

"We have to get truffles and persuade the mother pig."

"Yes, that's how we do it, let's get the truffles right away."

"Where then?" asks Hugo.

"Oh, I know another farm where a farmer secretly grows truffles. There are dogs there too. But…"

"But you're a fox," Hugo interrupts and grins, "...and you can secretly take some with you..."

"Actually, I'd have to dig them up first, but you got that one right, Hugo".


Two days later it was time.

Actually, the mother pig had accepted Frenchy's offer, she even squeaked with laughter because she was absolutely sure that her piggies would win the competition.

On those early mornings, when it was still very quiet on the farm, everyone was eager and ready for the competition to begin, but especially the piggies couldn't wait to get started.

But the puppies were also excited, because they knew they had to win today. On the other side the little piggies were quite sure of their cause, because they knew that their pig noses were certainly the better ones for finding truffles, they were pigs after all.

Unknown to most, Frenchy together with Hugo the boar had managed to gather the truffles. They had spent half the night carefully burying the little truffles around the farm. Secretly, he had buried most of them at the edge of the forest, because there the puppies already knew their way around.

In front of the excited group Frenchy stood on his hind legs. "Attention dear puppies and piggies. I'm going to count to three, then we're off, then you must find the truffles and bring them here, understand?"

The puppies and piggies nodded their little heads.

"One, two.....and three!"

As if struck by lightning, the piggies and puppies ran off in all directions.

They ran from corner to corner, from tree to tree, searching, snooping, and keeping their snouts low to the ground. Right from the beginning, the piggies started digging small holes in the ground with their snout.

After a few minutes the pigs had already dug up the first truffles. The little dogs also searched as fast as they could, but they were not sure if they were searching in the right place. They ran like crazy all over the place.

The mother dog cheered her offspring on with all her might, barking and shouting as loud as she could.

"Come on little ones, search faster, you can do it!"

Frenchy watched the snooping competition from the height of a fence, it seemed to him the little piggies somehow had a bit more experience with smelling.

After a few minutes, the piggies had already dug up five pieces, while the puppies thought they had found a small truffle in the bush.

It came as it had to come.

The piggies were quicker, and eventually, they found most of them. They laughed and squealed with excitement, while the dogs gathered sadly around the mother. Even the children of the farm, who were watching the spectacle from the fence, were a little sad because they loved the puppies too.

Sad and beaten, the doggies trotted back to the mother dog.

"Come on, little ones, there's nothing we can do."

Frenchy turns to Hugo. "Maybe we can do something."

"But the doggies have lost", Hugo objects.

"I have an idea. If it works, we all win."

The next morning before dawn, while the piggies were still sleeping, the farmer came and the troughs were filled, but Frenchy and his friends were already hiding behind the troughs, and when the man had finished his work they immediately grabbed some of the troughs and dragged them as fast as they could to the other side of the pigsty. Yet some of the filled troughs were left for the piggies. When the puppies saw the food coming they immediately ate as much and as fast as they could. And gogs can be very fast eaters, much faster than pigs! As soon as they had finished the puppies and friends dragged the troughs back to the pig's corner.

Of course there was a lot of noise in the pigsty, the piggies wondered, why half of the troughs were empty.

They started to complain and squeaked as loud as they could, actually they were all upset. Then Frenchy came and calmed them by waving his pawns. "Quiet piggies", he said. "As you can see, there is enough food for everybody. But we had to give some to the puppies."

"Why? They lost the competition?" The mother-pig intervened.

"That's right! They lost because the piggies are quicker and can probably smell a little better."

"Then why did you give them anything?" The mother pig wanted to know.

"Because, the first step to winning is getting up early, besides….sharing is caring."

**Frenchy and the Beaver**

On this beautiful but slightly rainy spring day Frenchy walks carefree through the forest and scurries happily from bush to bush and from tree to tree. Actually, Frenchy likes it when its raining, because then the forest smells so wonderful, somehow it seems as if the leaves, the ground and the whole air smells so beautifully of nature.

On the banks of a creek, Frenchy takes a break from walking. But when Frenchy looks down at the creek he can hardly believe his eyes. Where's the water? Just yesterday there was a deep stream of water, but now he only sees brown earth and a thin trickle of water, where the has the creek gone? That is impossible! After calming down a bit Frenchy decides to get to the bottom of the matter. He walks upstream because he wants to know where the water had disappeared first.

Frenchy only needs to walk a few minutes before he discovers the strangest thing he has ever seen. Across the creek some kind of a barrier seems to have been built. Hundreds of tree branches, small tree trunks and the remains of bushes have simply been laid across the water, creating a dark wall of squashed tree branches and thick stacked leaves. A real barrier and it looks like a dam. Amazed, Frenchy investigates the dam that interrupts the creek from the other side, so he carefully climbs the dam, he needs to find out who built this barrier, and what the heck was going on here, because whoever built this, had managed to stop the natural flow of the water! Frenchy can even spot some exhausted fish trying to get through the branches to the other side of the dam, but they can't make it, the dam is just too thick, and too many leaves and brushwood were clogged in between.

Some fish are already swimming very close to the barrier, they are zigzagging and Frenchy can see them trying to get through tiny openings, some are already poking their heads out of the water curiously to see what's going on.

Suddenly a huge shadow fights its way through the bushes. What was that? Over there again! A big animal seems to be stalking through the bushes, and now Frenchy can see it clearly, there's a strange animal lurking in the bushes, long like a dog, with thick smooth fur, a face like that of a marten or a racoon, and it has a strange big tail that is very flat. Suddenly the animal jumps into the water, dives and disappears. And then suddenly, Frenchy can hardly believe it, the creature shoots out of the water and jumps right in front of him.

The two animals look at each other in amazement.

"Who are you?" asks Frenchy.

"I'm the nice Beaver," says the unknown animal.

"What is a beaver," asks Frenchy.

"Oh, we are animals that live in the water and on land."

"And what is this barrier? Did you build it?"

"Oh, that's a dam, I built it with my wife, Bee."

"But you're not allowed to do that!"

"Why not?"

"The fish can't swim through!"

"But we need a dam, we are beavers."

"Why, what do you want with it?"

"Mainly we protect ourselves with it, we hide in the dam from dangerous animals."

French looks at the rodent skeptically. "Tell me, what kind of animal is dangerous for you beavers?"

"Well, eagles and foxes, for example."

Frenchy leaps forward. "I'm a fox!"

The beaver's eyes widen "Oh my goodness!", then he dives.

But after just a few minutes, he appears in the middle of the creek at a safe distance from the dam.

Frenchy stands on his hind legs. "Dear beaver, you don't need to be afraid of me or the foxes here in the forest."

"Why not? You're a fox, and foxes eat beavers."

"Not always," says Frenchy. "Here in this forest we are all friends, we all know each other here."

"You mean you won't hurt us beavers?"

Frenchy narrows his eyes, suddenly he has an idea. "It depends," he says.

"What is important? Can you guarantee our safety?"

Frenchy takes a few moments to answer. "… under one condition."

"Tell me your condition, please!"

You must make the dam smaller and leave a passage for the fish."

"For the fish?"

"Yes, so they can swim up and down the creek. And so that the water always flows naturally and therefore stays clean."

"And then you won't hurt us?"

Frenchy nods.

"And the other foxes remain peaceful with us beavers?"

"That I can pretty much guarantee," says Frenchy.

**The Burrow**

One of Frenchy's favorite spots in the woods is a small clearing that is right in the middle of the forest, actually where the woods are usually thickest.

It's a beautiful sunny spring morning, the leaves are still light green and the first insects such as dragonflies, bees and bugs are buzzing around. Frenchy is quiet happy because that is the secret place where he plans to meet his girlfriend Emma the goose later that day.

This is a special place because here the grass seems to grow higher and there are wild flowers everywhere, actually an ideal place to hide here with Emma.

Frenchy snoops the ground and suddenly it's all dark, what's going on here? Frenchy can hardly believe it, but he is staring into a very deep dark hole.

*Who did that*, Frenchy mumbles. Because this hole looks new, and he had never seen such a deep, dark hole here or anywhere.

Who could have dug such a hole? It wasn't one of his fox friends, that he would have known for a long time.

Had he just heard a noise, something like a slight wheeze? This had to be investigated now! Frenchy sticks his head into the hole, nothing to see. But something is rustling and shuffling down there. Carefully, crouching on one paw after the next,

Frenchy sneaks into the tunnel bit by bit. As it's almost completely dark in the tunnel, Frenchy suddenly sees reflective lights, and then he recognizes the lights, these are eyes!

"Who's there?" Frenchy asks loudly.

"Please don't hurt us," replies a hesitant voice.

Frenchy gets a little closer to the unknown creature.

"Oh, now I recognize you," says Frenchy. "You're a rabbit!"

And sure enough, a hare is lying crouched and huddled in front of him.

"Yes, I'm a rabbit and I'm here with my baby."

Directly behind the hare, Frenchy can now see a very small hare, which seems to be the daughter of the mother hare. "Now I'm curious," says Frenchy.

"Why are you hiding in this dark tunnel?"

"I built the tunnel this morning while the weather was still good," the rabbit replies.

"But why, the sun is shining outside."

"I'm an old rabbit, I know the weather can change quickly. Besides, we are safe here."

"Safe from who?"

"Well, for example from hunters."

"Oh, I know the hunter, he's definitely not coming here in the middle of the forest today."

"Nevertheless, it's safer here for me. And you're not going to hurt us, are you?"

"No, no way," Frenchy replies. "I'm just a curious fox"

"Well, then you can be our friend."

"And we can help each other," adds Frenchy. "I got to go now now, maybe we'll see each other again soon."

At that moment, Frenchy doesn't know how right he is.

Just when Frenchy climbs out of the tunnel thunder and lightning strikes the forest. As Frenchy looks up to the darkened sky the first raindrops are already dropping on his nose.

Seconds later, storm and rain is hitting the forest, Frenchy runs as fast as he can deeper into the forest, but no matter where he runs it rains everywhere!

*There's only one option in this weather*, Frenchy murmured, slightly disturbed.

Frenchy quickly jumps back into the deep hole where the rabbits live.

When the rabbit recognizes Frenchy, she starts laughing: "Now you know what friends are for, come in here!"

A few moments later, Frenchy sits comfortably with his new friends, the rabbit mother and her baby rabbit in the burrow; this is a dry place where he can wait until the weather gets better, or, who knows, maybe much longer.

## The Mink Farm

At first Frenchy thought a dog was coming, but he froze, because the animal in front of him was not a dog at all, what kind of animal was it? The unknown creature walked right up to Frenchy and stopped only a snout's length from Frenchy.

"Help me, please help me" said the unknown animal.

Frenchy took a step back and looked at the unknown creature. It probably had its size, a pointed face with very small ears, but it had an amazingly beautiful coat, in black-brown color, only the fur seemed much denser than his.

"You want my help," Frenchy asked. "Who are you anyway?"

"My name is Minki, and I'm a mink."

"I've never seen you before. Why do you need help?"

"I'm a fugitive."

"Fugitive? Where are you from?"

"All the way from the north, I've been on the road for many days."

Frenchy walks slowly around this strange creature. "No wonder, for I have never seen an animal like you."

"Am I safe here," asks the mink.

"By whom? I'm just a harmless fox," says Frenchy.

The mink starts to cry. "By the humans who captured my family."

"Excuse me? Tell me your story. Where is your family?"

"They locked up my whole family. On a farm."

"A farm?"

"My dad, my mom, my sister, and lots and lots of other minks. I think they call it a fur farm."

"And you want to see your family again, right?"

"Yes," cries the mink. "But I'm afraid to go back."

"Wait here," Frenchy says soothingly. "I'll get my friends, and then we'll go to this farm together, and we'll look for your family."

"Oh thank you, you're a lucky fox."

"I hope you will be lucky too. Don't move from the spot, see you later."

Determined and excited, Frenchy runs as fast as he can to the meadows on the edge of the forest. Here he is about to meet his friend Hugo the wild boar. When Hugo hears the story, he immediately offers his help. With his good sense of smell he could find out what happend to the mink's family, he thinks.

Frenchy runs to the next place to meet his friend Baloo, a small black bear who just makes himself comfortable in front of a bear den.

Baloo also has an excellent sense of smell, besides he is very strong, can run fast, and when it counts can be a real helper.

"Come friends," says Frenchy. "In the forest waits the little mink, together we will manage to find his family again."

Briefly, the mink is introduced to the friends, and off they march. Miki gives the direction, and the friends focus on their senses, snooping the ground, and keeping their ears pricked.

The next morning, they finally reach a large fence, but they can't see through it and it's very high.

"Someone is trying to hide something here," says Hugo, "can you jump up and see what's behind it?"

The little mink and Frenchy are good climbers and scurry to the top of the fence, from here they have a excellent view. At first they can only see dark barracks, but what the two see next leaves them speechless

Between two trees, on a long rope hang hundreds of mink furs, all laid side by side, but only furs and no bodies. There is no trace of living minks.

Little Minki screams as loud as he can, "Mommy, Daddy!"

Completely shocked, Frenchy tells his friends what he saw, while the mink keeps screaming, "Where are you, where are you?"

Suddenly they hear a different scream, it's more a kind of a howling, a scary sound they had never heard before in their lives.

Little Minki yells, "There, on the truck!"

Frenchy and the friends can hardly believe it. A truck is slowly driving between the barracks. And in the back of the truck-bed is a big cage. The cage similar to a those seen in a circus. And behind the bars they can recognize a group of minks, some waving at them, actually making all kinds of noises and movements to attract attention.

The little mink jumps up and down, then shouts: "Look there! There are my parents in the cage!"

"My God, they're still alive then," says Hugo.

"Yes, now we have to find a way to free them," adds Baloo.

Frenchy nods, "I think I have an idea, but we have to hurry!"

Frenchy runs ahead of the truck and then immediately returns. "Hugo, there's the gate up ahead around the bend, that's where the truck has to go through!"

"So?"

"You run there, and stand in front of the truck, when the truck honks, you stay there, don't let the truck pass you!"

"Oh, you want me to stop the truck?"

"Yes, and you can stand on your hind legs too, then you make the people in the truck laugh."

Hugo nods. "I think I can do that."

Frenchy turns to Baloo. "Okay, while the people are distracted by Hugo, you sneak up behind the truck and smash the door open with your mighty paws."

"Oh yes, I can do that."

"Then let's go, hurry up!"

The friends run off, and as agreed, Hugo the wild boar stands directly in front of the truck at the camp exit. The truck honks like crazy, but then it stops.

With a mighty swipe that shakes the whole cage Baloo smashes the door open.

Frenchy yells, "Out, all minks out! You are free!"

Completely distraught, the minks flee the truck, running in all directions.

"Mom, Dad this way," yells little Minki, the family barely has time to hug when Frenchy pushes them:

"Hurry up, the men are already getting out of the truck, run as fast as you can into the forest!"

The chaos is great, but all minks make it to the forest. The truck almost hit Hugo, but even a truck doesn't stand a chance against a wild boar that's running away quickly.

Eventually the minks actually managed to escape to the far north where they are able to set up a new home, but that's another story.

**Walking on Thin Ice**

The first spring air suggested that winter seemed to be over soon.

But part of the forest was still covered in snow, and the ice on the lake was still frozen, or so it seemed.

For Frenchy the fox, who at the time was a still bit younger, it was the first winter he ventured onto the ice.

Sometimes he saw children with their parents on the ice, they skated, some older children raced across the ice on skateboards.

This is what Frenchy wanted to imitate, and when he saw that a child put the skateboard aside for a moment to rest, French just grabbed the scateboard, and quick as a weasel, raced at full speed across the ice . Now, that was the sensation, the children were thrilled as they had never seen a fox on a skateboard before. Surprisingly, Frenchy could do it much faster than most children, he was even quicker than the running dogs!

However, on this early spring morning, all the children ventured onto the ice with their skates and skateboards, they figured today was the last day the winter-ice would hold.

From the looks of it, the ice still seemed thick near the shore, but towards the middle of the lake the ice was already making noises, it started to creak and crack. The parents told the children to be carefully, and most of the children only ventured onto the ice very cautiously and only near the short.

Frenchy wanted to help, just in case; he stood on the ice on the middle of the lake so that the children wouldn't come here, because he thought here the ice was just too thin for a human, but not for a fox, because a small fox like Frenchy weights only a few pounds.

That's why Frenchy hissed at the children when they got too close to the thin ice. But then a very brave, or rather careless little boy, who couldn't even skate properly, moved unconcerned to the middle of the lake, he didn't seem to hear or to understand the warnings of the little fox.

Frenchy stood on his legs right in front of the boy.

And the boy just laughed and walked further out onto the thin ice without paying attention.

Frenchy whistled between his teeth a loud as he could, he even stood on his hind legs, and circled the boy, Frenchy tried desperately and by all means to influence the carefree boy, while at the edge of the forest, his friends watch the hustle and bustle, they too were concerned, as the ice creaked louder by the minute.

Suddenly, Rollo the wolf appeared out of the woods, he ran right to the middle of the lake.

"You've come at the right time," said Frenchy. "Now we can howl together!"

They sat down right in front of the boy, blocking his way. Both Frenchy and the wolf started to howl with all their strength, actually it sounded like a whole wolfpack.

The boy stopped and gazed in amazement at the animals.

Then, suddenly, on the shore of the lake, people appeared, they were screaming and waving their arms. A little confused the boy scratched his head and then he turned around, he first looked at the animals, then he started screaming *Mama, Papa, I am here*!

Then, as if struck by lightning, the little boy ran towards his parents.

The other children became scared as well and started to run off the ice as fast as they could.

"The children are safe for today," said Rollo to Frenchy.

Frenchy nodded. "Which means we don't have to come back."

"Not this year", Rollo replied.

## The Bird's Nest

Frenchy the fox was very fond of birds, especially when he was very young. At that time, when he was still little and inexperienced, he was always looking for a nest on a tree or sometimes a hedge, where there would be young birds hiding. He then would carry them home, not thinking that the little animals would much rather be in their little nest, which their mama had so carefully built for them.

Actually, Frenchy once found a bird's nest in which there were four little birds. Frenchy hid in the bush and waited until the mother left to get food, after all he did not want to frighten the mother. The truth is, foxes are normally feared by birds, although with

Frenchy they had nothing to fear at all; because Frenchy was a friend of the animals, and he had never eaten a bird. No, Frenchy loved birds, he loved their singing and tweeting. When the little birds were alone, he took the young ones out of their little nest and carried them home. But one day when the bird mother returned she found her nest empty! She cried desperately, she thought something had happened to the little birds! At once she flew around everywhere to look for them. Eventually she flew over an open field at the edge of the forest where she heard suspicious chirping. She immediately swooped down and recognized her dear little ones that were hidden in the bushes.

Frenchy was totally perplexed when he saw the big bird.

"Oh, give me back my little birds!" The mother bird begged Frenchy. "I want to carry them back home to their nest"

"Why you want to do that", Frenchy asked.

"There in the nest I'll spread my wings over them and in the evening I sing my birds a song, because then they fall asleep quickly. Bring them back to me!"

When Frenchy heard how much the mother bird begged for her young ones, he immediately gave them back, and she carried one after the other on her beak back, and flew them home to her warm little nest.

Frenchy was curious, so he visited the little birds quite often and even brought them some food. The mother bird was grateful for this and eventually they became friends, the mother bird even visited Frenchy once in a while and sometimes even sang him a song. And actually that was all frenchy wanted from the birds.

**Frenchy and the Squirrel**

Frenchy was wandering through the deep forest as he often does, looking for food, and also perhaps to meet some of his friends. Just when he took a short break, and just as he was making himself comfortable and preparing for a nap, he suddenly felt a short pain, something hard had hit him on the head. Startled, he stood up, but saw nothing. Again, something hit him, this time on his back.

He locked to the ground and saw what looked like a pine cone or a stick.

But then he heard a giggle, he looked around in surprise. And what he saw next he could hardly believe. A squirrel was standing on a branch at the top of the tree and throwing small pine cones at him.

"Hey squirrel, I don't like that at all," Frenchy scolded.

But the squirrel just laughed, ripped another pinecone off the branch and threw it with a great swing at Frenchy, who just managed to jump to the side. "Stop it," Frenchy yelled at the still-laughing squirrel.

But the squirrel seemed to have a lot of fun throwing things at Frenchy. Frenchy saw how the squirrel broke another pine cone of the branch. Now he's had enough, this went definitely too far. As if struck by lightning, Frenchy jumped onto the first branch, from there he jumped higher from branch to branch until he reached the squirrel. Now the squirrel stopped laughing. Terrified, it retreated to where the branch was getting thinner and thinner.

But Frenchy did not stop, slowly he got closer to the animal.  "So now you're scared, aren't you?"

"Oh you're a fast fox, you don't want to hurt me?"

Frenchy can't help but showing his sharp teeth.

"Didn't you hear me when I warned you?"

"Yes, but I thought you'd stay on the ground."

Frenchy shook his head. "Now I'm here."

The squirrel was really scared now. "Please don't eat me, please don't eat me!"

"Put down the pine cone," Frenchy demanded.

The squirrel dropped the pine cone at once. "You don't want to hurt me, do you?"

"No, I won't," said Frenchy, "but you can't throw things at me again, because that can hurt, you know that?"

"I didn't even think about that," replied the squirrel.

"Listen, if you bother me again, I will tell all my friends in the forest that you are disturbing the peace here."

"Who are your friends?"

"I will tell you. For example my friend Emma the goose or Charlie the crow, but some of my friends are of course foxes, and they are bigger than me and much faster than me. And they all might come and get you."

The squirrel whined. "What can I do? It's in my nature to throw things and play around."

"Okay I get that, but why don't you try to do something positive with your temper?"

"What can I do?"

Frenchy scratched his head. "I think I have an idea. You will collect nuts and pine cones and store them in the deep forest, and if you find a piece of meat you will carry it with you."

"And then what", asked the squirrel.

"Okay, if you see me, you can throw the piece of meat at me, but you have to throw the met to my feet, do you understand?"

"Yes, but what do you want with the meat."

"Well, I eat the meat myself and safe some for my friends."

Suddenly the squirrel started crying.

"What's going on now?" asked Frenchy.

"I want to be your friend too. But I don't want to have to do anything for it."

"You don't have to," Frenchy replied. "Just tell me your name."

"Jimmy, I'm Jimmy the squirrel."

"Okay Jimmy, tomorrow I'm going into the woods with you and I'll introduce you to my friends."

"Tomorrow?"

"Yes, and I assume by then you have collected some nice pieces of meat for my friends."

**Barking Dogs**

It must have been the middle of autumn, because during those days it rained heavily every day. In fact, large parts of the forest became one swamp, and all the animals sought dry shelter. But for many animals there just weren't enough dense bushes and nests to really stay dry all the time, so Frenchy, Hugo the wild hog, Emma the goose, and Bambi the deer finally found a barn, a remote farmhouse. They made it dead he farm together and were really glad that they were saved from the weather. In fact, they had just made themselves comfortable on the straw when two dogs ran in through the open barn door. They weren't particularly big, didn't look dangerous either, but they were very quick and above all loud.

They stood in front of the friends and barked as loud as they could.

Frenchy and Hugo tried to convince them to be quiet as good as they could, but the dogs were kept barking like hell, they just didn't understand what these strangers wanted here on their turf.

Frenchy and his friends retreated behind the fence to have a secret discussion

Finally they decided on a plan. Despite the weather Emma flies around the barn, checks every corner of the farmhouse.

Comes back with a bag in her mouth, the friends find delicious chunks in there, eat them,

Now the dogs start barking again.

Frenchy speaks to the dogs: "Who wants one of these?...."

But the dogs only bark again.

Then Frenchy throws a few of the chunks to their feet, they immediately jump on them, but in the last second Frenchy throws the clubs away, he puts them directly in front of Hugo the wild boar. Then all the friends hold their hands and paws in front of their mouths. Frenchy explains. "You get those to eat only when you are quiet!"

The dogs look at each other

Both dogs swarm briefly and nod their heads.

"Finally they seem to understand," says Hugo, relieved.

"Let's make a circle," says Frenchy.

Even the dogs understand it, to line up in his circle.

Then Frenchy throws a few of the tasty chunks at the feet of all the animals."

After they all have finished their meals, the dogs sit quietly, now they look attentively at Frenchy, maybe there is more to understand?

Frenchy nods to everyone. "So, it's true. It is so with animals as well as with humans. Sitting together and sharing food makes us friends and understand each other."

See the new book:

The Adventures Frenchy the Little Red Fox and his Friends

# Frenchy and the Wolves

# Frenchy the Fox, the Girl and her Dogs

# The Polluted Lake

# Frenchy Rides the School Bus

# Frenchy and the Marten in the Attic

# The Secret Winter Path

…and many more stories in text and pictures.

Get you latest edition of the **_Frenchy the Fox Kids Book Series_**, available on all major book platforms.

\*\*\*

www.ingramcontent.com/pod-product-compliance
Lightning Source LLC
Chambersburg PA
CBHW071812160426
43209CB00003B/59